WRITING JAPANESE KATAKANA

An Introductory Japanese Language Workbook

JIM GLEESON

TUTTLE Publishing

Tokyo | Rutland, Vermont | Singapore

"Books to Span the East and West"

Tuttle Publishing was founded in 1832 in the small New England town of Rutland, Vermont [USA]. Our core values remain as strong today as they were then—to publish best-in-class books which bring people together one page at a time. In 1948, we established a publishing outpost in Japan—and Tuttle is now a leader in publishing English-language books about the arts, languages and cultures of Asia. The world has become a much smaller place today and Asia's economic and cultural influence has grown. Yet the need for meaningful dialogue and information about this diverse region has never been greater. Over the past seven decades, Tuttle has published thousands of books on subjects ranging from martial arts and paper crafts to language learning and literature—and our talented authors, illustrators, designers and photographers have won many prestigious awards. We welcome you to explore the wealth of information available on Asia at www.tuttlepublishing.com.

Published by Tuttle Publishing, an imprint of Periplus Editions (HK) Ltd.

www.tuttlepublishing.com

Text © 1996, 2015 Jim Gleeson

LCC Card No. 2004111447
ISBN 978-4-8053-1350-3
This edition first published, 2015

This title was first published in 1996 as *Introduction to Written Japanese Katakana*.

Distributed by:

Japan	North America, Latin America & Europe	Asia Pacific
Tuttle Publishing	**Tuttle Publishing**	**Berkeley Books Pte. Ltd.**
Yaekari Building, 3rd Floor	364 Innovation Drive	3 Kallang Sector #04-01
5-4-12 Osaki, Shinagawa-ku	North Clarendon,	Singapore 349278
Tokyo 141 0032	VT 05759-9436 U.S.A.	Tel: (65) 6741-2178
Tel: (81) 3 5437-0171	Tel: 1 (802) 773-8930	Fax: (65) 6741-2179
Fax: (81) 3 5437-0755	Fax: 1 (802) 773-6993	inquiries@periplus.com.sg
sales@tuttle.co.jp	info@tuttlepublishing.com	www.tuttlepublishing.com
www.tuttle.co.jp	www.tuttlepublishing.com	

27 26 25 24   10 9 8 7 6 5   2405VP
Printed in Malaysia

TUTTLE PUBLISHING® is a registered trademark of Tuttle Publishing, a division of Periplus Editions (HK) Ltd.

It is widely accepted that students of Japanese progress more quickly if they learn the written component of the language at an early stage of their studies. Unfortunately, many students are daunted by the task of learning a large number of seemingly complex characters.

The complexity of Japanese characters, however, is something of an illusion, for many of the characters are merely combinations of comparatively few elements. This fact becomes apparent as one progresses through the two forty-eight character syllabaries, known collectively as kana, and the two thousand or so kanji characters that are used in written Japanese today.

Anybody who is able to master English, with its irregular spellings and idiosyncratic pronunciations, is more than equipped to master written Japanese.

The hiragana and katakana syllabaries are purely phonetic characters, which function much like the letters of the English alphabet. In this respect, kana are quite different from kanji characters, which are based on Chinese ideographs and which represent ideas.

The katakana syllabary is used primarily to represent borrowed words (from languages other than Chinese), although it is also used for botanical names and is sometimes used in place of hiragana or kanji for emphasis. In some ways, the use of katakana in Japanese parallels the use of italics in English. Onomatopoeic words and other expressive terms are also generally written in katakana, although hiragana can also be used.

As katakana is used to write foreign words that often contain sounds not found in Japanese, katakana has a number of apparent irregularities. Instead of providing a detailed description of the irregularities, this book adopts the approach of simply noting the irregularities as they occur and allowing the student to become familiar with the use of katakana through the numerous practice examples.

Each of the hiragana and katakana syllabaries represents all of the sounds in spoken Japanese. Unlike kanji, which can take on a variety of pronunciations according to their context, the pronunciation of the kana characters is quite regular. Although it is possible to write Japanese using only katakana, a native Japanese speaker would find it somewhat difficult to understand. Kanji are used for clarity, eloquence, and immediacy of meaning. It is customary for the student to write using only the kana at first, then to substitute kanji into their writing as the

ハジメニ

kanji are learned. Katakana, however, continues to be used when writing words of a foreign origin.

Japanese schoolchildren learn their characters by writ-ing them out, and this is generally acknowledged as the fastest way to master them.

This book has been prepared so that students at the introductory level of Japanese can become acquainted with the written component of the language in the quickest possible way. The overriding priority has been given to active student involvement, with a variety of practice sentences and expressions provided to reinforce the characters learnt at each stage of progress. The book also features grayed-out, trace-over characters to enable the student to gain the correct feel and balance of each character.

This book uses the Hepburn system of romanization. It is important to remember, however, that Japanese is a separate language with an independent set of sounds to English, and hence, any attempt to romanize it can only be an approximation.

Contents モクジ

ツカイカタ

In both printed and handwritten Japanese, the characters occupy imaginary squares of equal size, with each character centered within its square.

All of the writing practice in this book involves writing characters within squares, and the squares have centerlines to provide the correct balance and feel for writing Japanese.

Traditionally, Japanese is written with a brush or *fude*, and this fact is reflected in many typographic styles today. Although the *fude* is no longer widely used, some principles of using a *fude* still apply to writing Japanese with a pencil or ballpoint pen — in particular, the stroke endings.

The strokes of Japanese characters terminate in one of three ways, as illustrated below.

i) Jumping, to produce a hook at the end of the stroke. This ending is called *hane*, from the verb *haneru*, to jump.
ii) Bringing the pen or pencil to a stop while it is on the page. This ending is called *tome*, from the verb *tomeru*, to stop.
iii) Lifting the pen or pencil off the page while it is moving. This ending is called *harai*, meaning 'sweep.'

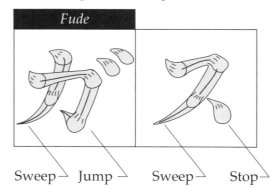

Fude

Sweep — Jump — Sweep — Stop

When tracing over the characters, be sure to keep these three types of stroke endings in mind, observing how the strokes of the gray-tinted characters terminate.

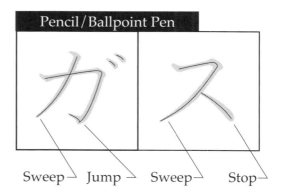

Pencil/Ballpoint Pen

Sweep — Jump — Sweep — Stop

In Japanese, as in English, there are many differences between handwritten and typeset characters. To enable students to gain the correct feel for written Japanese, educators in Japan have developed a neutral typeface which incorporates the features of handwritten Japanese without the stylistic idiosyncracies of any individual.

This typeface is known simply as Schoolbook or *Kyōkasho*, and is the standard typeface used to teach Japanese schoolchildren the written language. All of the practice characters in this book are set in *Kyōkasho*.

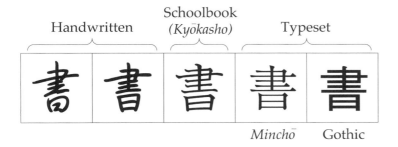

To provide familiarity with a range of type variations, each character entry in this book is accompanied by four different character styles, as shown below. These variations are included for recognition only.

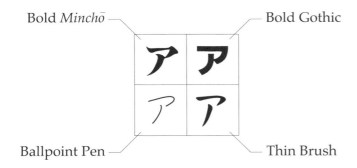

The upper left variation is a bold *Mincho* typeface while the upper right variation is a bold Gothic typeface. Typefaces of this kind are frequently used in advertisements and newspaper headlines.

The lower left typeface simulates the characters written with a ballpoint pen, while the lower right typeface is a thin brush script indicative of that used on traditional occasions.

In around 100 A.D., Chinese characters, known as kanji, entered Japan via the Korean peninsula. Since that time, many thousands of kanji have come to Japan, many of them falling into disuse or becoming obsolete. Today, there are about two thousand kanji in general use, with several thousand more being used on special or formal occasions.

Although kanji refer to ideas or objects, by around 800 A.D., a special set of kanji had evolved which were used for their pronunciation, with the innate meaning of the characters being discarded.

In the Heian period (794–1185), these characters underwent a series of simplifications and reductions as the Buddhist priests abbreviated the characters when annotating the holy scriptures.

The result was a simplified set of characters based on kanji, but in many cases, with a portion of the character discarded. Unlike kanji, which refer to ideas or objects and which can take on a variety of pronunciations according to their context, each katakana character is pronounced in only one way, and there is no conceptual meaning.

A chart showing the evolution of all the katakana characters is given inside the front cover.

1500 B.C.	Chinese tortoise shell inscription
202 B.C.	Chinese Kan era
C100 A.D.	Kanji entered Japan.
350 A.D.	Kanji in wide-spread use
540 A.D.	Buddhism came to Japan.
794 A.D.	Heike Clan came to power. Kyoto established as imperial capital.
Heian period	Various art forms flourished.
1185 A.D.	Heike Clan defeated in battle.
Present	Character forms remain virtually unchanged after Heian period.

Buddhist priests develop kanji shorthand.

Kanji

Katakana

カタカナ

a	i	u	e	o
ア	イ	ウ	エ	オ

ka	ki	ku	ke	ko
カ	キ	ク	ケ	コ

sa	shi	su	se	so
サ	シ	ス	セ	ソ

ta	chi	tsu	te	to
タ	チ	ツ	テ	ト

na	ni	nu	ne	no
ナ	ニ	ヌ	ネ	ノ

ha	hi	fu	he	ho
ハ	ヒ	フ	ヘ	ホ

ma	mi	mu	me	mo
マ	ミ	ム	メ	モ

ya		yu		yo
ヤ		ユ		ヨ

ra	ri	ru	re	ro
ラ	リ	ル	レ	ロ

wa		o		n
ワ		ヲ		ン

ア

a

1 2

アア
アア

アアアア ア ア

ア ア ア

ア ア

イ

i

1 2

イイ
イイ

イイイイ イ イ

イ イ イ

イ イ

ウ

u

1 2 3

ウウ
ウウ

ウウウウ ウ ウ

ウ ウ ウ

ウ ウ

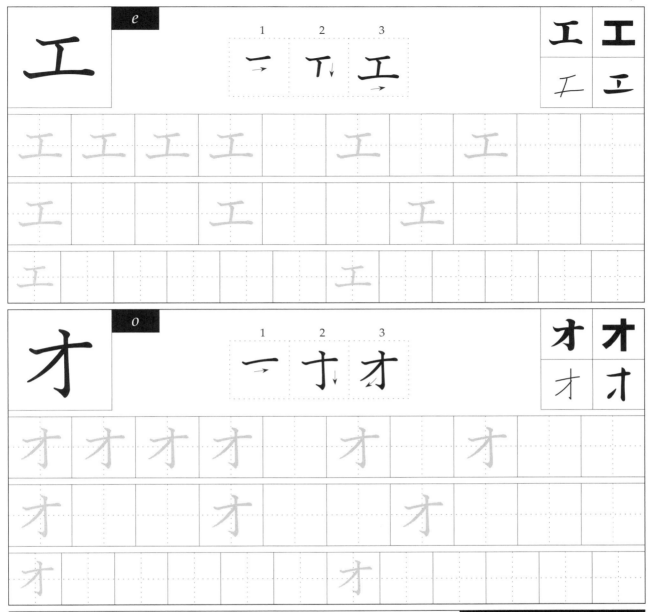

The Lengthening Character

Long vowel sounds are represented in katakana by a horizontal stroke. This character can be used after any katakana character, except the voiced consonant *n* and the particle *o*. In the case of the five characters on these pages, the lengthening character is written and romanized as follows:

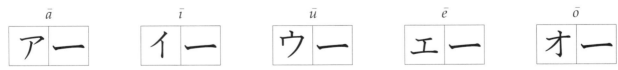

Special Combinations

The katakana character *u* is combined with the following characters to give 'w' sounds which occur in loanwords, but which do not occur naturally in Japanese. These are contracted sounds and are pronounced as a single syllable.

wi	*we*	*wo*
ウィ	ウェ	ウォ

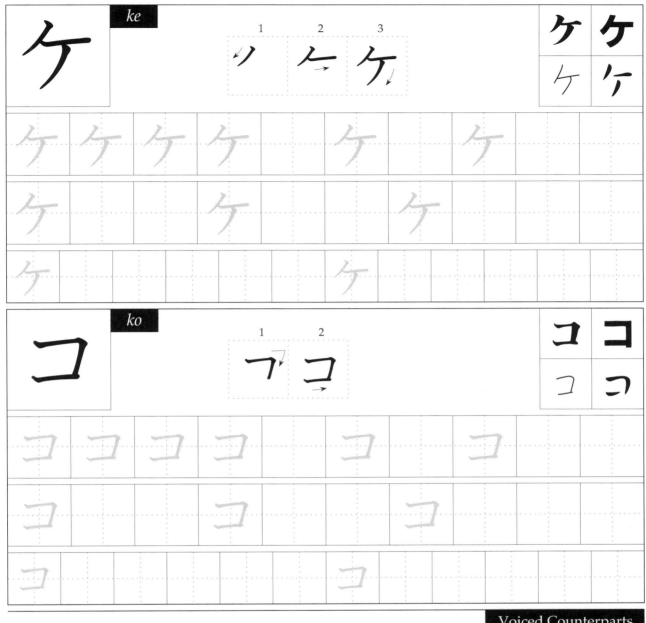

Voiced Counterparts

The characters *ka, ki, ku, ke* and *ko* have the following voiced counterparts:

ga	*gi*	*gu*	*ge*	*go*
ガ	ギ	グ	ゲ	ゴ

Practice

kāki iro – khaki (color)

カーキ イロ

kuēkā – Quaker

クエーカー

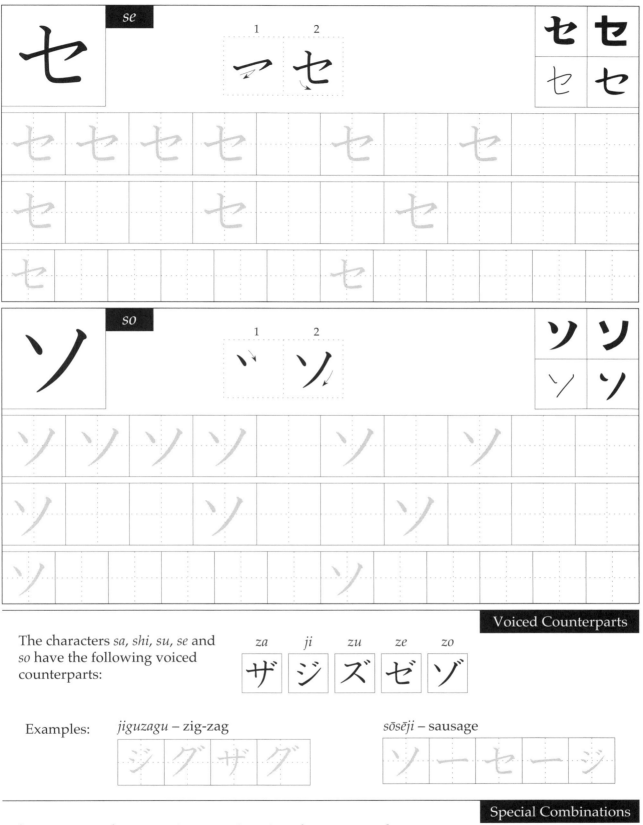

Voiced Counterparts

The characters *sa*, *shi*, *su*, *se* and *so* have the following voiced counterparts:

za	ji	zu	ze	zo
ザ	ジ	ズ	ゼ	ゾ

Examples:

jiguzagu – zig-zag

ジ	グ	ザ	グ

sōsēji – sausage

Special Combinations

The katakana character *shi* is combined with *e* to give the following sounds that occur in loanwords, but which do not occur naturally in Japanese. These are contracted sounds and are pronounced as a single syllable.

she		je	
シ	エ	ジ	エ

15

kuizu – quiz

クイズ

kokoa – cocoa

ココア

sōsu – (Worcestershire) sauce

ソース

akua – aqua

アクア

sukoa – score

スコア

saizu – size

サイズ

gāze – bandage, gauze

ガーゼ

Suisu – Switzerland

スイス

ēsu – ace (tennis, playing cards, etc.)

エース

sukuea – square

スクエア

kēki – cake

ケーキ

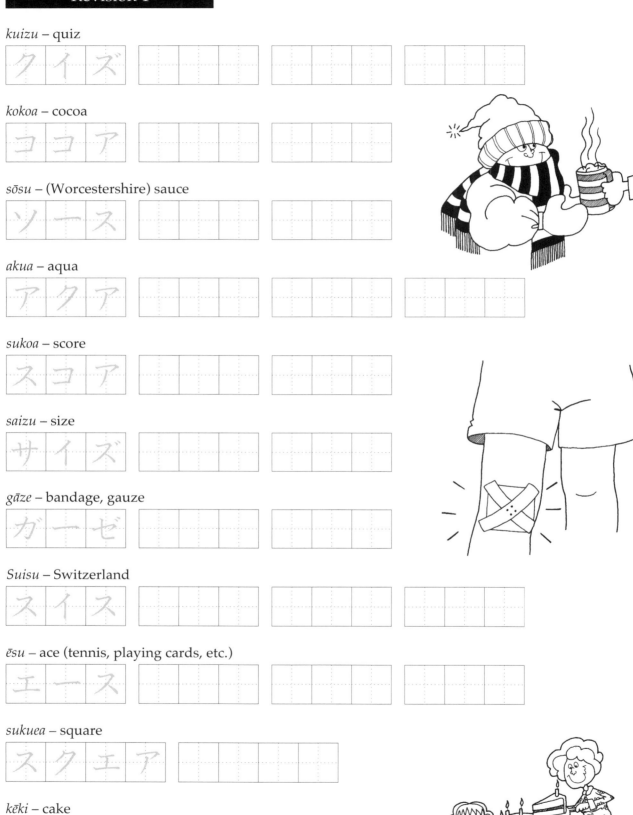

okē – okay

オーケー

ēkā – acre

エーカー

sākasu – circus

サーカス

shīsō – seesaw

シーソー

kēsu – case

ケース

kisu – kiss

キス

oashisu – oasis

オアシス

sukaiburū – sky blue

スカイブルー

kīui – kiwi

キーウィ

sukī – skis, skiing

スキー

sukīuea – skiwear

スキーウエア

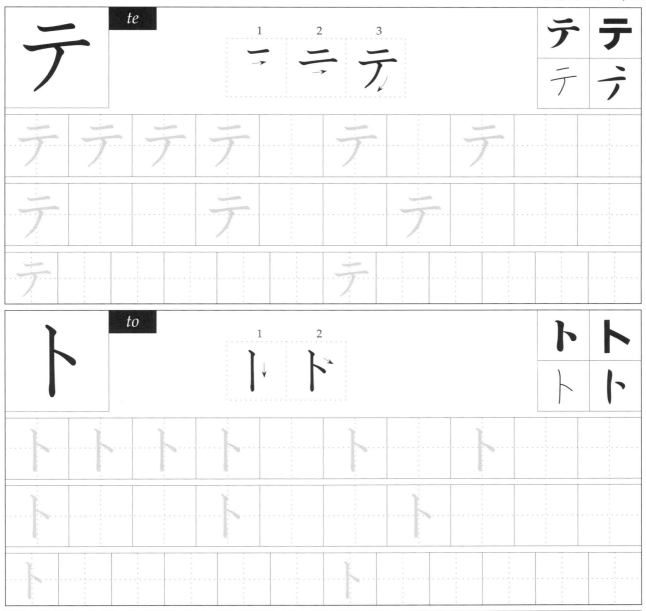

As with hiragana, the small katakana character *tsu* ッ indicates a glottal stop, which is romanized by the doubling of the subsequent character.

English short vowel sounds are often rendered in katakana with a glottal stop, as in the example at the right.

The Glottal Stop – ッ

suicchi – switch

スイッチ

The characters *ta, chi, tsu, te* and *to* have the following voiced counterparts:

Voiced Counterparts

da	*ji**	*zu**	*de*	*do*
ダ	ヂ	ヅ	デ	ド

* ヂ and ヅ are rarely used. The *ji* and *zu* sounds in loanwords are written ジ and ズ.

The characters *chi* and *te* occur in the special combinations shown at the right to give sounds which occur in loanwords, but which do not occur naturally in Japanese. These are contracted sounds and are pronounced as a single syllable.

Special Combinations

che	*ti*	*di*
チェ	ティ	ディ

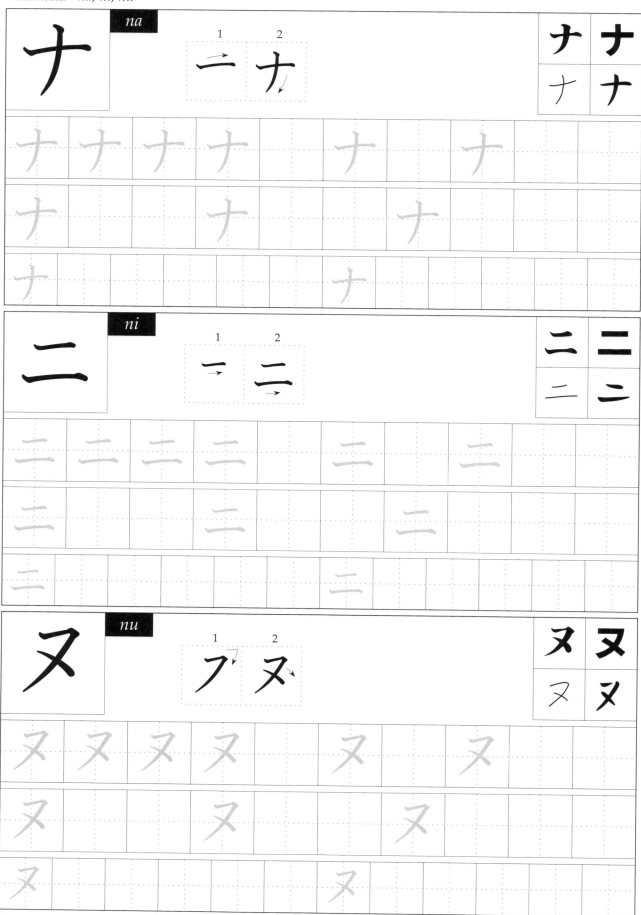

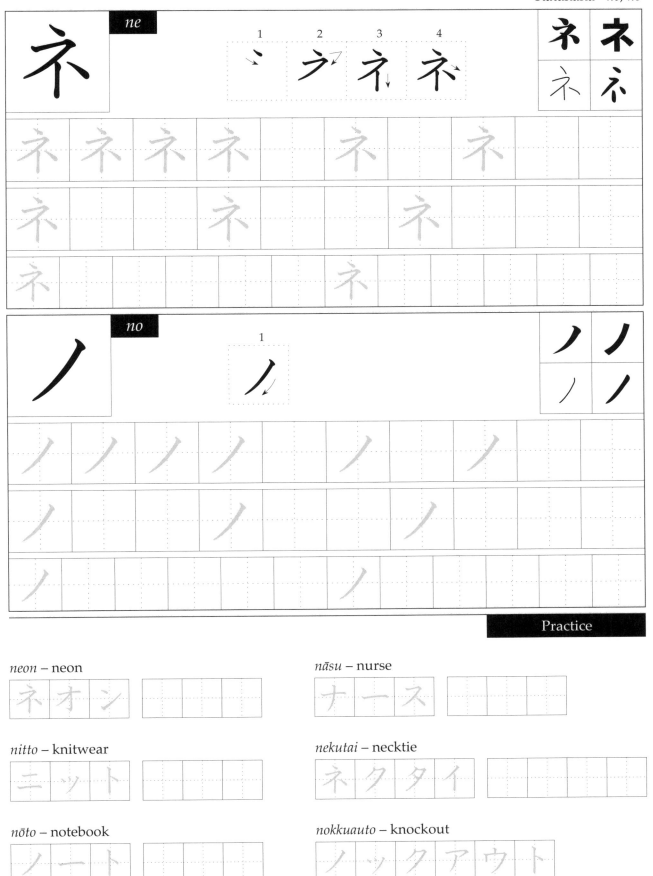

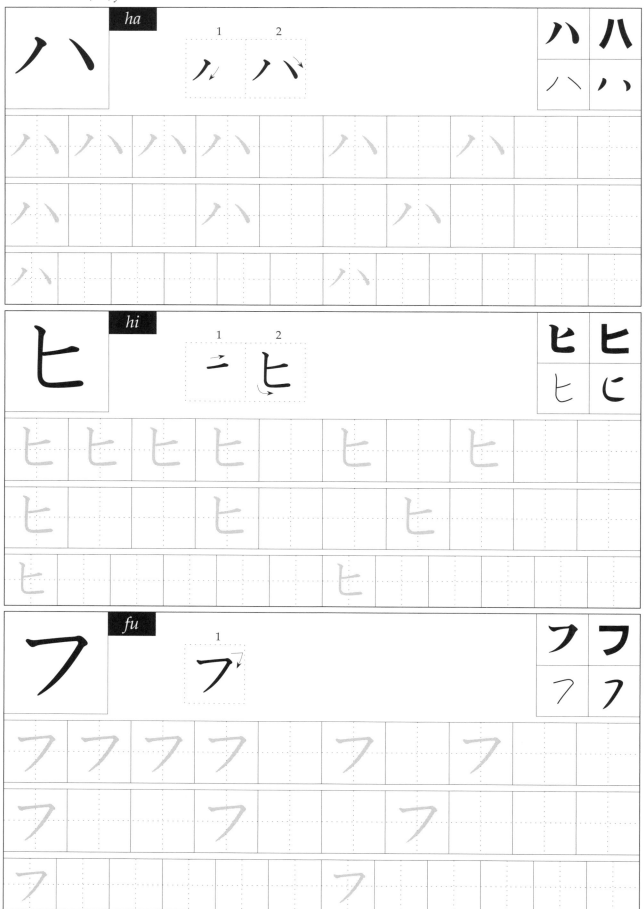

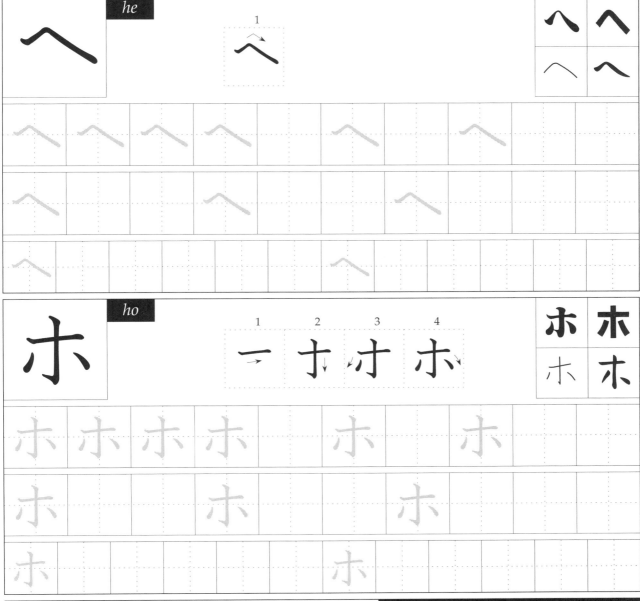

The characters *ha, hi, fu, he* and *ho* have the following voiced and semi-voiced counterparts:

Voiced:						Semi-voiced:				
ba	*bi*	*bu*	*be*	*bo*		*pa*	*pi*	*pu*	*pe*	*po*
バ	ビ	ブ	ベ	ボ		パ	ピ	プ	ペ	ポ

The katakana character *fu* is combined with *a, i, e,* and *o* to give the following sounds which occur in loanwords, but which do not occur naturally in Japanese. These are contracted sounds and are pronounced as a single syllable.

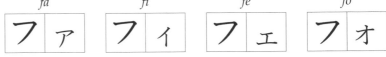

fa		*fi*		*fe*		*fo*	
フ	ァ	フ	ィ	フ	ェ	フ	ォ

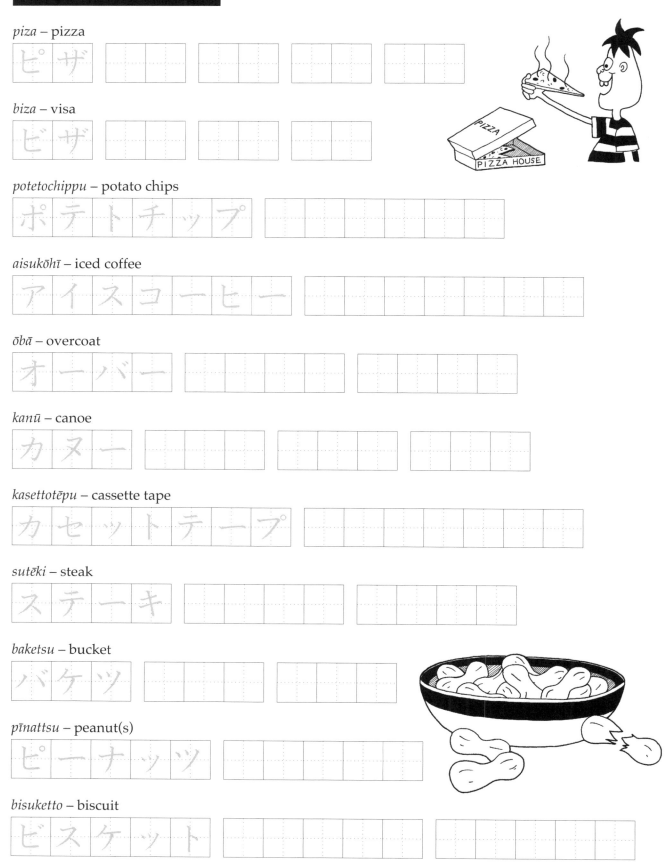

piza – pizza

ピザ

biza – visa

ビザ

potetochippu – potato chips

ポテトチップ

aisukōhī – iced coffee

アイスコーヒー

ōbā – overcoat

オーバー

kanū – canoe

カヌー

kasettotēpu – cassette tape

カセットテープ

sutēki – steak

ステーキ

baketsu – bucket

バケツ

pīnattsu – peanut(s)

ピーナッツ

bisuketto – biscuit

ビスケット

kapuchīno – cappucino

カプチーノ

haikā – hiker

ハイカー

tekisuto – textbook

テキスト

batā – butter

バター

takushī – taxi

タクシー

dēta – data

データ

chīzu – cheese

チーズ

bideo – video

ビデオ

katto – cut

カット

ākēdo – arcade

アーケード

oisutā – oyster

オイスター

Dābī – Derby

ダービー

ōē – OA (office automation)

オーエー

akusesu – access

アクセス

sētā – sweater

セーター

gitā – guitar

ギター

daibā – diver

ダイバー

ōboe – oboe

オーボエ

kāpetto – carpet

カーペット

tāgetto – target

ターゲット

daietto – diet

ダイエット

ōsodokkusu – orthodox

オーソドックス

ōnā – owner

オーナー

basu – bus

バス

tsuā – tour

ツアー

taipu – type, pattern

タイプ

batto – bat

バット

sepia – sepia

セピア

banana – banana

バナナ

sōda – soda, carbonated drink

ソーダ

ōtobai – motorbike

オートバイ

kībōdo – keyboard(s)

キーボード

ōbahīto – burnout

オーバーヒート

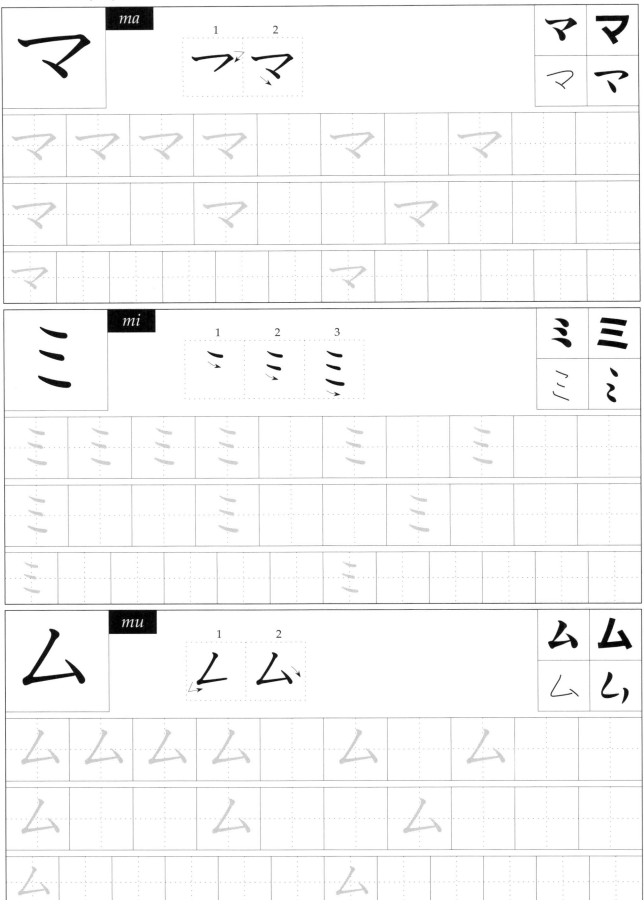

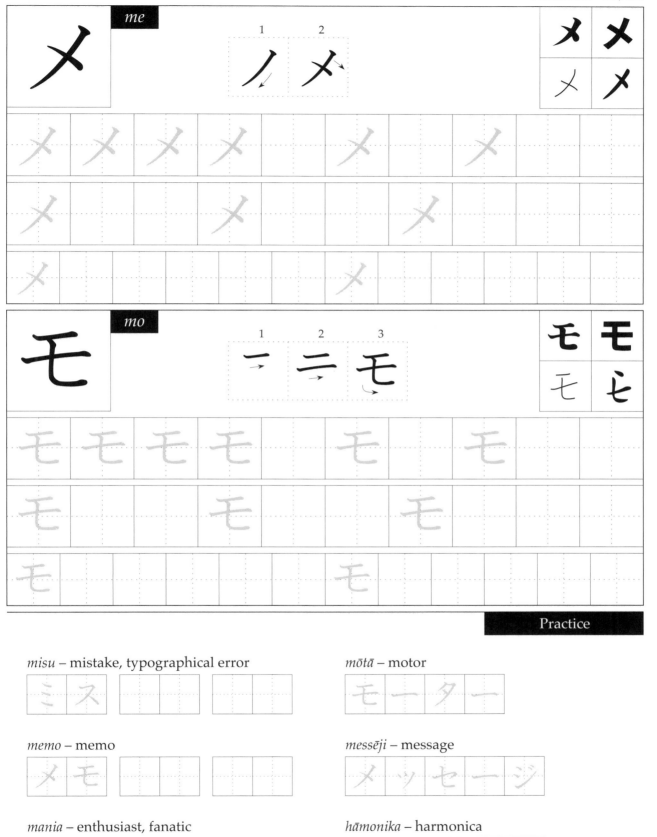

misu – mistake, typographical error

mōtā – motor

memo – memo

messēji – message

mania – enthusiast, fanatic

hāmonika – harmonica

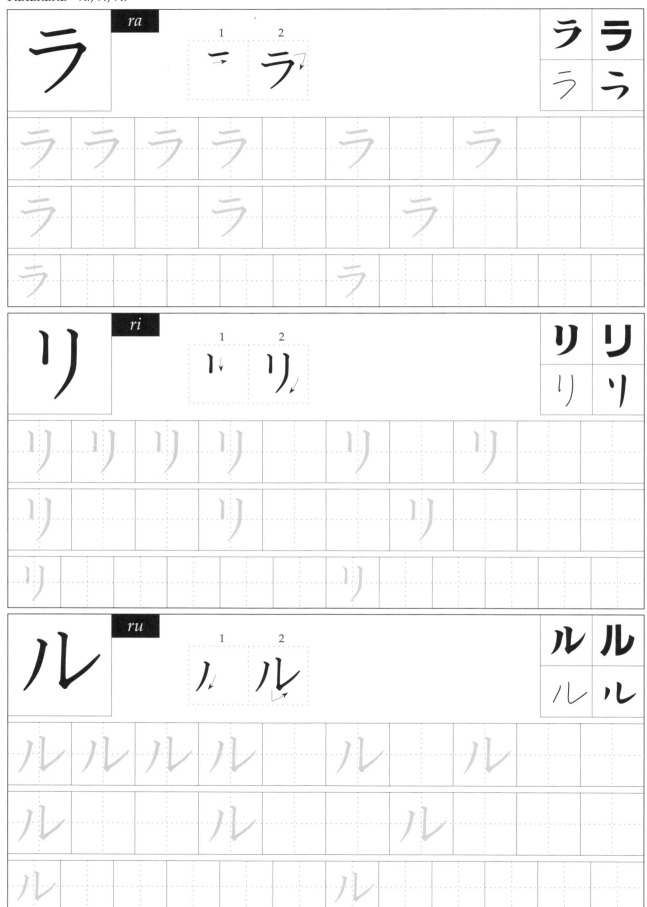

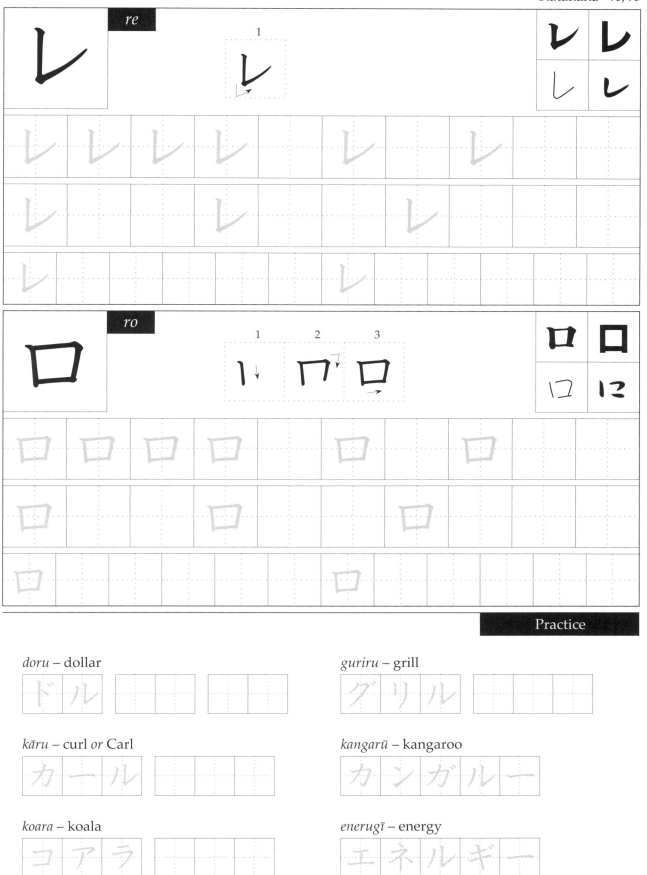

Practice

doru – dollar

guriru – grill

kāru – curl *or* Carl

kangarū – kangaroo

koara – koala

enerugī – energy

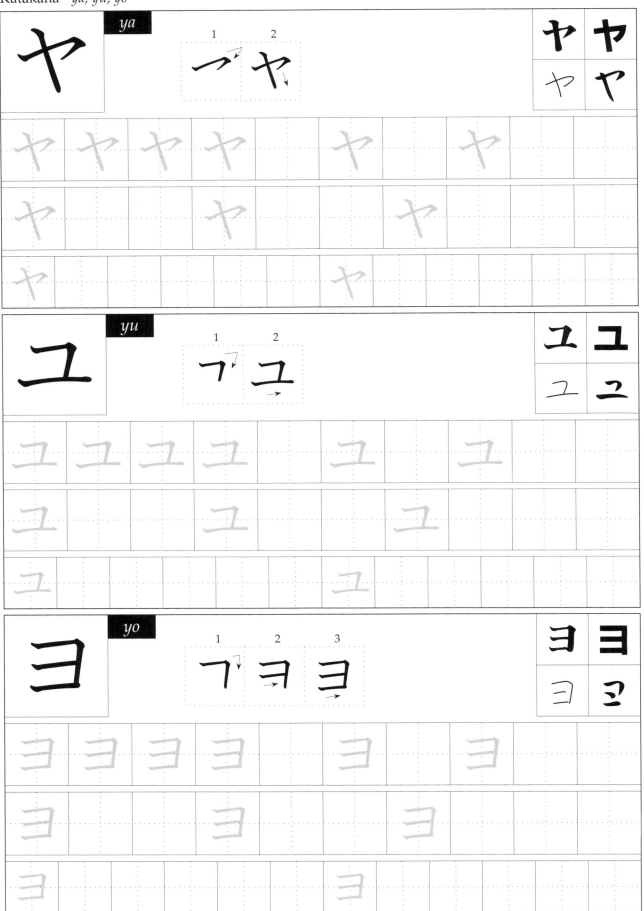

shawā – shower

シャワー

intānashonaru – international, American

インターナショナル

akushon – action (movie)

アクション

kyasuto – cast (of characters)

キャスト

kyasshukādo – ATM card, bank card

キャッシュカード

sukejūru – schedule

スケジュール

rasshuawā – rush hour, peak hour

ラッシュアワー

gyararī – gallery

ギャラリー

kyaria – career

キャリア

jānarisuto – journalist

ジャーナリスト

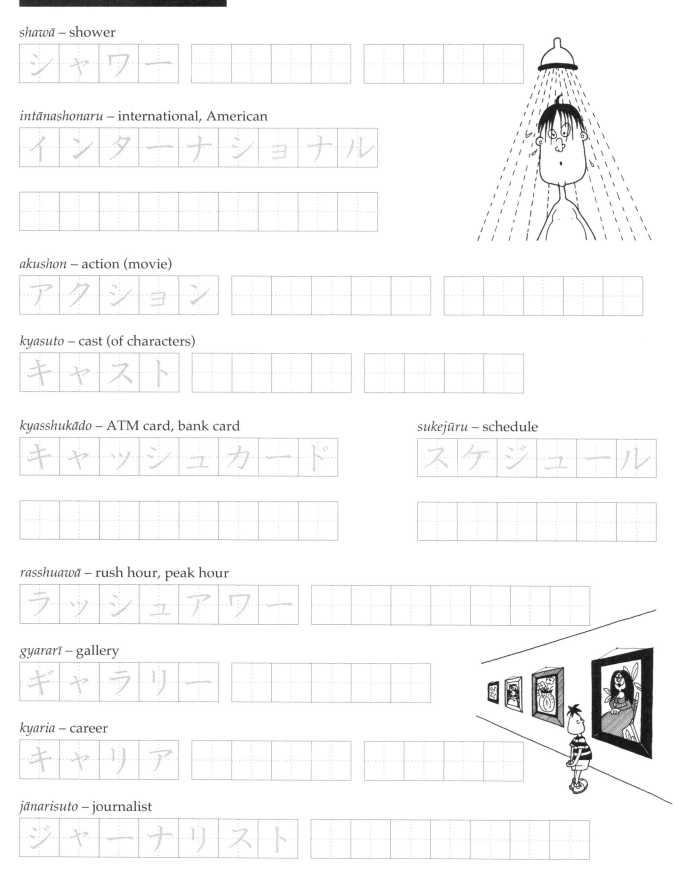

intabyū – interview

インタビュー

shattā – shutter (window *or* camera)

シャッター

nyūsu – news

ニュース

kontakutorenzu – contact lens

コンタクトレンズ

hyūzu – fuse

ヒューズ

chokorēto – chocolate

チョコレート

intāchenji – interchange

インターチェンジ

ōkesutora – orchestra

オーケストラ

myūjikaru – (stage) musical

ミュージカル

jūsu – juice, uncarbonated soft drink

ジュース

karutetto – quartet

カ ル テ ッ ト

kyanpasu – campus

キ ャ ン パ ス

kajuaru – casual

カ ジ ュ ア ル

karendā – calendar

カ レ ン ダ ー

komāsharu – (TV / radio) commercial

コ マ ー シ ャ ル

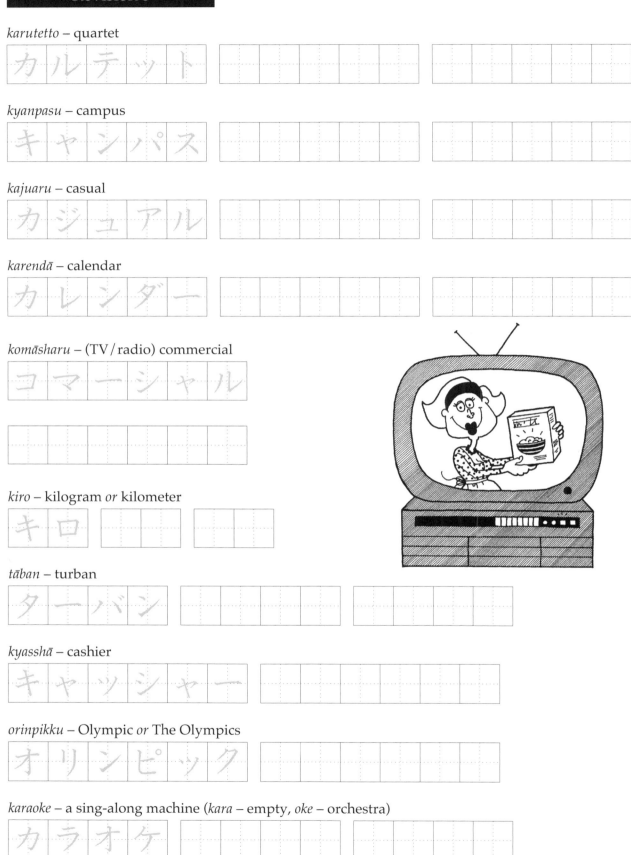

kiro – kilogram *or* kilometer

キ ロ

tāban – turban

タ ー バ ン

kyasshā – cashier

キ ャ ッ シ ャ ー

orinpikku – Olympic *or* The Olympics

オ リ ン ピ ッ ク

karaoke – a sing-along machine (*kara* – empty, *oke* – orchestra)

カ ラ オ ケ

konpyūta – computer

コ ン ピ ュ ー タ

karuchāshokku – culture chock

カ ル チ ャ ー ショ ッ ク

opera – opera

オ ペ ラ

karā – color

カ ラ ー

kyabia – caviar

キ ャ ビ ア

kāsoru – cursor

カ ー ソ ル

kyanpēn – (advertising) campaign

キ ャ ン ペ ー ン

kuraianto – client

ク ラ イ ア ン ト

gārikku – garlic

ガ ー リ ッ ク

boryūmu – (sound) volume

ボ リ ュ ー ム

Special Combinations

As noted in the text, katakana characters occur in special combinations to accommodate sounds in loanwords which do not occur naturally in Japanese. These are contracted sounds and are pronounced as a single syllable. Examples of words that use these special combinations are given below.

wi ウィ *we* ウェ *wo* ウォ

Dāwin – Darwin

ダ ー ウ ィ ン

Noruwē – Norway

ノ ル ウ ェ ー

Suwēden – Sweden

ス ウ ェ ー デ ン

Wōkuman – Walkman

ウ ォ ー ク マ ン

Gōrudenwīku – Golden Week holidays (April 29 – May 5)

ゴ ー ル デ ン ウ ィ ー ク

mineraruwōtā – mineral water

ミ ネ ラ ル ウ ォ ー タ ー

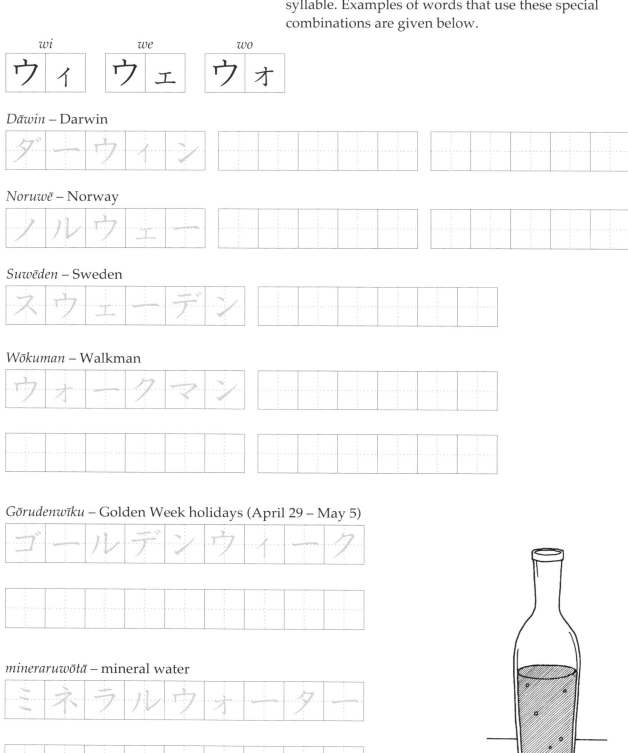

she

シ	ェ

je

ジ	ェ

jettokōsutā – roller coaster

ジ	ェ	ッ	ト	コ	ー	ス	タ	ー

purojekuto – project (n.)

プ	ロ	ジ	ェ	ク	ト

Shēkusupia – Shakespeare

シ	ェ	ー	ク	ス	ピ	ア							

shefu – chef

シ	ェ	フ										

che

チ	ェ

chero – cello

チ	ェ	ロ						

chesu – chess

チ	ェ	ス					

fa	*fi*	*fe*	*fo*
ファ	フィ	フェ	フォ

fasshon – fashion

ファッション

firumu – (a roll of) film

フィルム

pafe – parfait

パフェ

fōku – fork

フォーク

infomēshon – information

インフォメーション

fenikkusu – Phoenix

フェニックス

fakkusu – fax

ファックス

fikushon – fiction

フィクション

kafeore – café au lait

カフェオレ

ti *di*

テ ィ デ ィ

borantia – charity work

ボ ラ ン テ ィ ア

tishatsu – T-shirt

テ ィ ー シ ャ ツ

ōdio – audio

オ ー デ ィ オ

direkutā – director

デ ィ レ ク タ ー

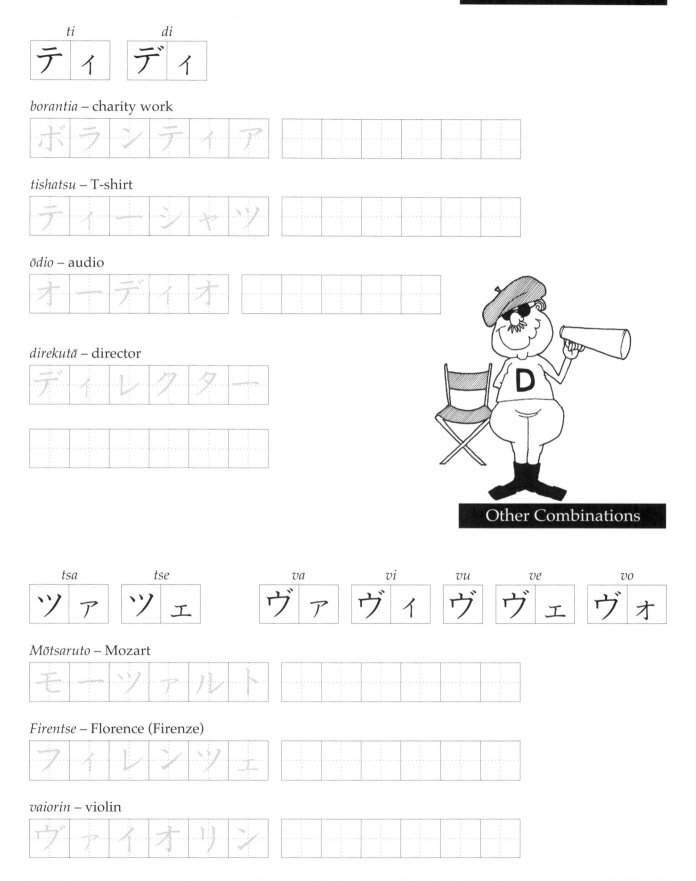

Other Combinations

tsa *tse* *va* *vi* *vu* *ve* *vo*

ツ ァ ツ ェ ヴ ァ ヴ ィ ヴ ヴ ェ ヴ ォ

Mōtsaruto – Mozart

モ ー ツ ァ ル ト

Firentse – Florence (Firenze)

フ ィ レ ン ツ ェ

vaiorin – violin

ヴ ァ イ オ リ ン

Non-English Loanwords

Due to the close relationship between Japan and America, most of Japan's loanwords today are of English origin. Nevertheless, foreign words have been incorporated into the Japanese language from different countries for the past four hundred years.

In the sixteenth century, the Portuguese came to Japan and introduced bread (*pan*), cigarettes (*tabako*), and deep-fried fish and vegetables (*tempura*). *Tempura* has become assimilated into Japanese and is usually written in hiragana. In the seventeenth century, the Dutch came to Japan introducing such things as coffee and beer.

After the Meiji Restoration in 1867, loanwords from different parts of Europe became part of the Japanese language. Many words concerning art and fashion entered Japanese from French, while many musical terms came from Italian. German was the source of a range of medical and philosophical terms.

These pages present a short list of Japanese loanwords that are not English in origin.

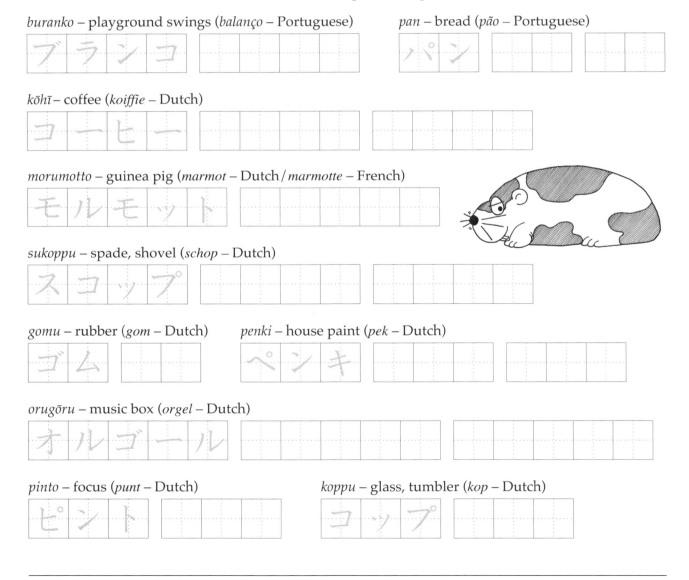

buranko – playground swings (*balanço* – Portuguese)

ブランコ

pan – bread (*pão* – Portuguese)

パン

kōhī – coffee (*koiffie* – Dutch)

コーヒー

morumotto – guinea pig (*marmot* – Dutch / *marmotte* – French)

モルモット

sukoppu – spade, shovel (*schop* – Dutch)

スコップ

gomu – rubber (*gom* – Dutch)

ゴム

penki – house paint (*pek* – Dutch)

ペンキ

orugōru – music box (*orgel* – Dutch)

オルゴール

pinto – focus (*punt* – Dutch)

ピント

koppu – glass, tumbler (*kop* – Dutch)

コップ

ankēto – questionnaire (*enquête* – French)

アンケート

pīman – green pepper (*piment* – French)

ピーマン

zubon – trousers (*jupon* – French)

ズボン

shūkurīmu – cream puff (*chou à la crème* – French)

シュークリーム

atorie – artist's studio (*atelier* – French)

アトリエ

arubaito – part-time work (*Arbeit* – German)

アルバイト

gerende – ski slope (*Gelände* – German)

ゲレンデ

tēma – theme, topic (*Thema* – German)

テーマ

zekken – athlete's bib, racing number, saddlecloth (*Decken* – German)

ゼッケン

rentogen – X-ray (*Röntgen* – German)

レントゲン

konsento – power point, wall socket (origin unknown)

コンセント

biru – building, office block

ビル

bīru – beer

ビール

manshon – Western-style apartment (steel and concrete construction)

マンション

apāto – Japanese-style apartment (timber construction)

アパート

panpusu – pumps (shoes)

パンプス

ponpu – (mechanical) pump

ポンプ

garasu – glass (as a substance)

ガラス

gurasu – glass, tumbler

グラス

sutoraiku – (baseball) strike

ストライク

sutoraiki – (labor) strike

ストライキ

mēta – meter, gauge, dial

メーター

mētoru – meter (unit of measurement)

メートル

baree – ballet

バレエ

barēbōru – volleyball

バレーボール

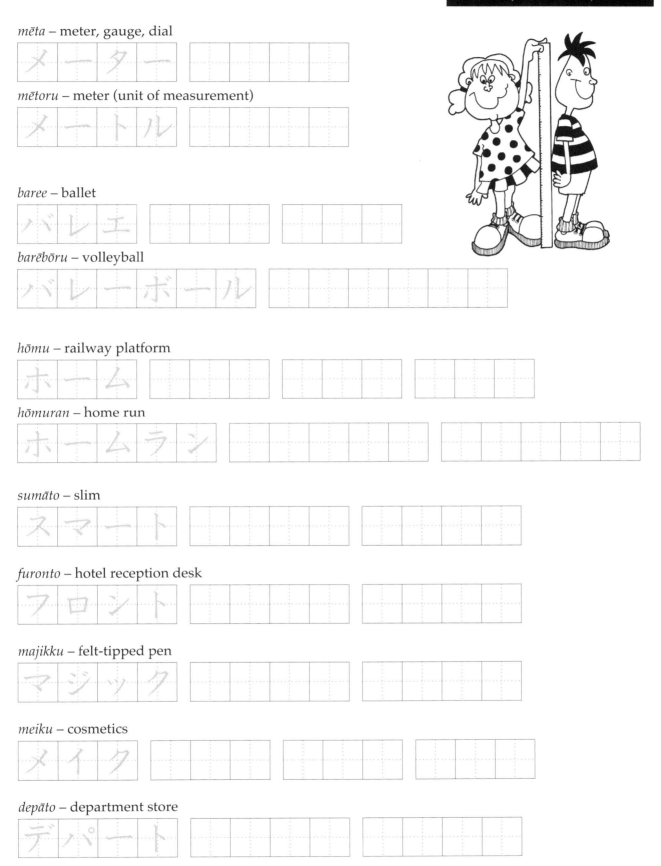

hōmu – railway platform

ホーム

hōmuran – home run

ホームラン

sumāto – slim

スマート

furonto – hotel reception desk

フロント

majikku – felt-tipped pen

マジック

meiku – cosmetics

メイク

depāto – department store

デパート

Idiomatic Terms

ōpunkā – convertible, cabriolet

オ ー プ ン カ ー

aidoru – popular famous person

ア イ ド ル

tarento – TV personality

タ レ ン ト

taimurīhitto – (baseball) RBI single hit

タ イ ム リ ー ヒ ッ ト

gurōbu – baseball glove *or* boxing glove

グ ロ ー ブ

kūrā – air conditioner

ク ー ラ ー

mēruadoresu – e-mail address

メ ー ル ア ド レ ス

waishatsu – (business) shirt

ワ イ シ ャ ツ

mēkā – manufacturer

メ ー カ ー

nōtacchi – no involvement

ノ ー タ ッ チ

kameraman – photographer

カ メ ラ マ ン

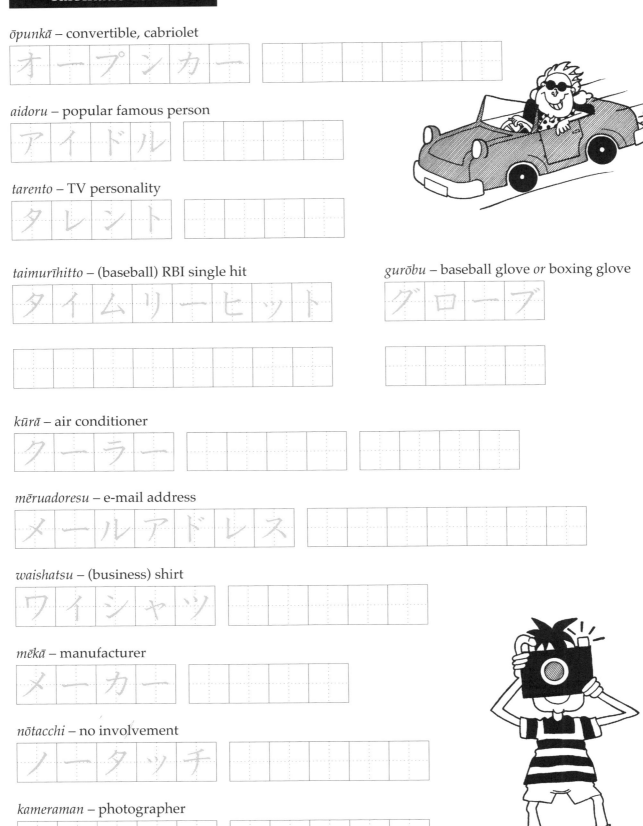

naitā – night game

ナ イ タ ー

mishin – sewing machine

ミ シ ン

renji – electric stove

レ ン ジ

terebi – television

テ レ ビ

tōsuto – sliced bread *or* toast

ト ー ス ト

pasokon – personal computer

パ ソ コ ン

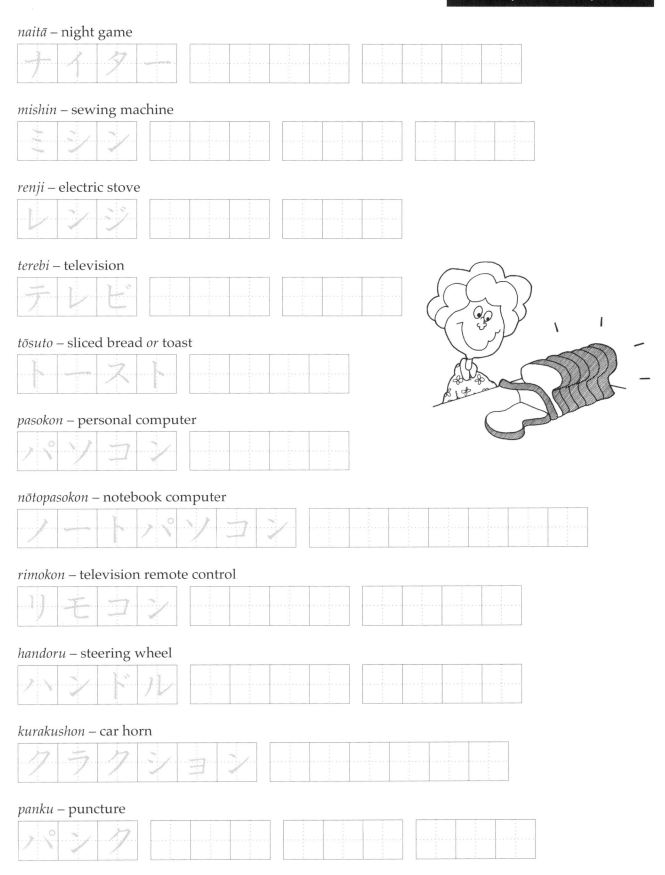

nōtopasokon – notebook computer

ノ ー ト パ ソ コ ン

rimokon – television remote control

リ モ コ ン

handoru – steering wheel

ハ ン ド ル

kurakushon – car horn

ク ラ ク シ ョ ン

panku – puncture

パ ン ク

chin – the bell of a microwave oven

チ　ン

pachiri – the click of a camera shutter

パ　チ　リ

gachan – glass or crockery breaking

ガ　チ　ャ　ン

pacchin – the click of a switch

パ　ッ　チ　ン

batan – a door slamming

バ　タ　ン

poron poron – the strumming of a guitar

ポ　ロ　ン　ポ　ロ　ン

joki joki – scissors snipping

ジ　ョ　キ　ジ　ョ　キ

riririrīn – a telephone ringing

リ　リ　リ　リ　ー　ン

dokān – a cannon or fireworks booming

ド　カ　ー　ン

pīpō – a siren screaming

ピ　ー　ポ　ー

chikutaku – a clock ticking

チクタク

buku buku – water boiling

ブクブク

paka paka – a horse galloping

パカパカ

gururūrū – a stomach rumbling

グルルルー

kī – the screeching of chalk on a blackboard, tires, etc.

キー

kyu kyu kyu – squeaking, such as when cleaning glass

キュキュキュ

basha basha – legs kicking in a swimming pool

バシャバシャ

pyon pyon – a rabbit hopping

ピョンピョン

hyū – the wind blowing

ヒュー

gabu gabu – a person gulping

ガブガブ

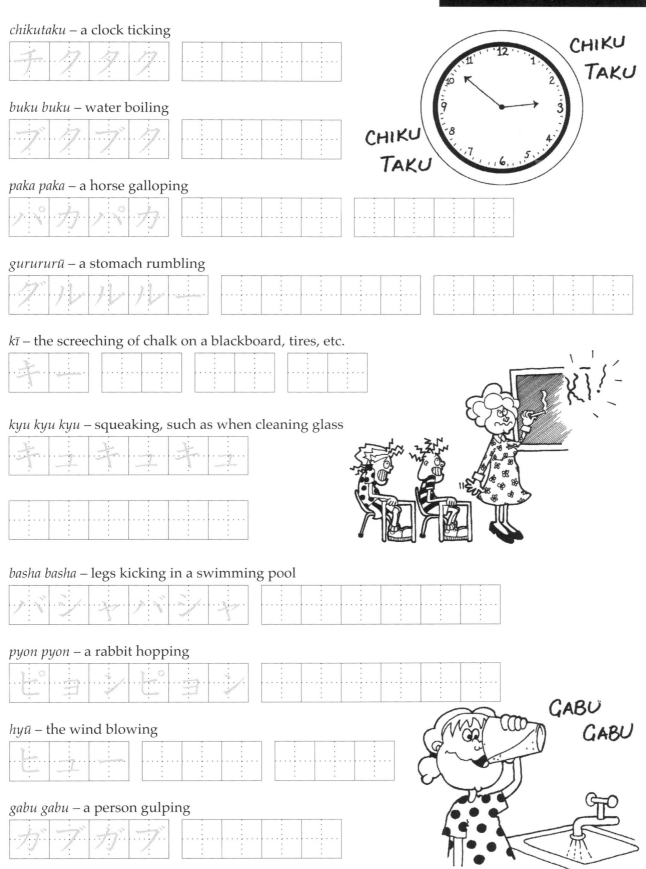

CHIKU TAKU

CHIKU TAKU

KĪ!

GABU GABU

HAKKUSHON !

hakkushon – a person sneezing

ハックション

kira kira – twinkling or sparkling

キラキラ

pika pika – shining, gleaming or flashing

ピカピカ

goshi goshi – a scrubbing brush scrubbing

ゴシゴシ

niko niko – smiling, all smiles

ニコニコ

doki doki – a heart beating

ドキドキ

DOKI DOKI

hihīn – a horse neighing

ヒヒーン

kakīn – a baseball bat striking a ball

カキーン

kokekokkō – a rooster crowing

コケコッコー

MUSHA MUSHA

musha musha – somebody chewing

ムシャムシャ

poppō – a steam train puffing

ポッポー

pinpon – a doorbell ringing

ピンポン

chū chū – a mouse squeaking

チューチュー

giko giko – a saw cutting

ギコギコ

mō mō – a cow mooing

モーモー

gaō – a lion roaring

ガオー

jā – water gushing out of a tap

ジャー

kero kero – a frog croaking

ケロケロ

kusha kusha – the crumpling of paper

クシャクシャ

kā kā – a crow squawking

カーカー

pata pata – a bird's wings flapping

パタパタ

shīn – silence

シーン

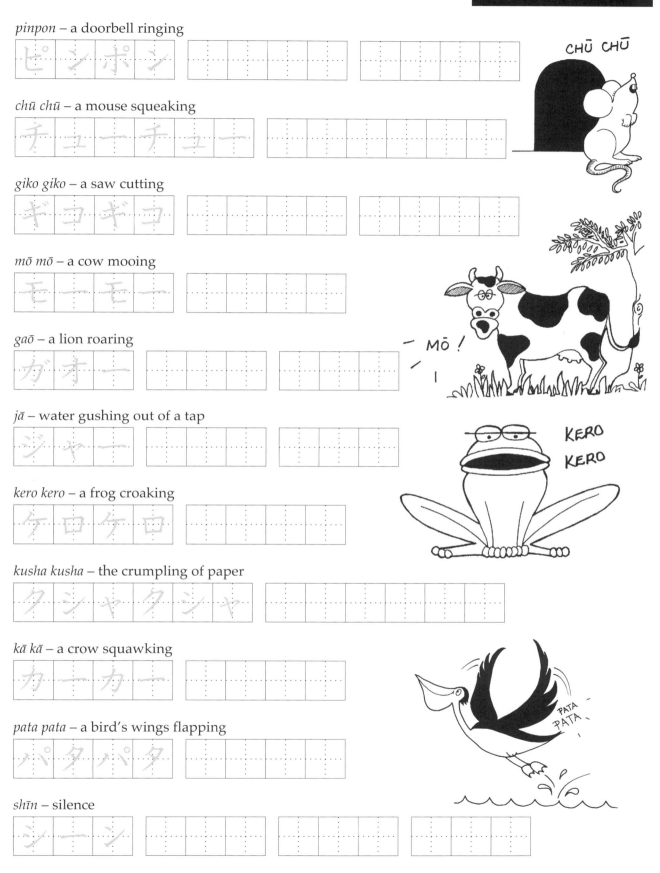

メニュー

① メニュー

② テリヤキバーガー

③ チキンバーガー

④ ダブルバーガー

⑤ ハンバーガー

⑥ チーズバーガー

⑦ フィッシュバーガー

⑧ フライドポテト

⑨ チキンナゲット

⑩ シェーク

⑪ アイスクリーム

⑫ ホットポテトパイ
ホットアップルパイ

⑬ コーラ
レモネード
ウーロンチャ

⑭ アイスコーヒー
アイスティー
オレンジジュース

⑮ コーンスープ
コーヒー
ホットチョコレート

On page 52 is a menu from a hamburger shop.

Look at the menu, then translate the terms into English. The numbers on this page correspond to the terms on the opposite page.

1. メニュー _____

2. テリヤキバーガー _____

3. チキンバーガー _____

4. ダブルバーガー _____

5. ハンバーガー _____

6. チーズバーガー _____

7. フィッシュバーガー _____

8. フライドポテト _____

9. チキンナゲット _____

10. シェーク _____

11. アイスクリーム _____

12. ホットポテトパイ _____

    ホットアップルパイ _____

13. コーラ _____

    レモネード _____

    ウーロンチャ _____

14. アイスコーヒー _____

    アイスティー _____

    オレンジジュース _____

15. コーンスープ _____

    コーヒー _____

    ホットチョコレート _____

Oribia – Olivia

Ashurī – Ashley / Ashleigh

Madison – Madison

Hanna – Hannah

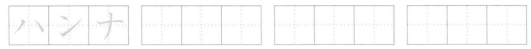

Sēra – Sarah

Rōren – Lauren

Samansa – Samantha

Izabera – Isabella

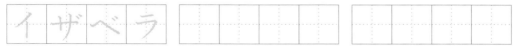

Emirī – Emily

Jeshika – Jessica

Sofia – Sophia

Sutefanī – Stephanie

ステファニー

Jenifā – Jennifer

ジェニファー

Natarī – Natalie

ナタリー

Kairī – Kylie

カイリー

Kuroe – Chloe

クロエ

Kyasarin – Catherine / Katherine

キャサリン

Nikōru – Nicole

ニコール

Maria – Maria

マリア

Jasumin – Jasmine

ジャスミン

Reicheru – Rachel

レイチェル

Juria – Julia

ジュリア

Andoryū – Andrew

アン ド リュー

Jeikobu – Jacob

ジェ イ コ ブ

Samyueru – Samuel

サ ミュ エ ル

Diran – Dylan

ディ ラ ン

Benjamin – Benjamin

ベン ジャ ミ ン

Gaburieru – Gabriel

ガ ブ リ エ ル

Jasutin – Justin

ジャ ス ティ ン

Kurisutofā – Christopher

ク リ ス ト ファ ー

Hose – Jose

ホ セ

Zakarī – Zachary

ザ カ リ ー

Robāto – Robert

ロ バ ー ト

Tōmasu – Thomas

トーマス

Arekisandā – Alexander

アレキサンダー

Jon – John

ジョン

Nikorasu – Nicholas

ニコラス

Raian – Ryan

ライアン

Maikeru – Michael

マイケル

Josefu – Joseph

ジョセフ

Ansonī – Anthony

アンソニー

Wiriamu – William

ウィリアム

Dēbiddo – David

デービッド

Jēmuzu – James

ジェームズ

North America

Amerika – America

アメリカ

Washinton – Washington

ワシントン

Atoranta – Atlanta

アトランタ

Map labels:
アラスカ
カナダ
バンクーバー
オタワ　ケベック
アメリカ
トロント　モントリオール
　　　　ボストン
シカゴ　ニューヨーク
デトロイト　ワシントン
サンフランシスコ
ロサンゼルス
アトランタ
ヒューストン
マイアミ
メキシコ
メキシコシティー

Bosuton – Boston

ボストン

Shikago – Chicago

シカゴ

Sanfuranshisuko – San Francisco

サンフランシスコ

Rosanzerusu – Los Angeles

ロサンゼルス

Maiami – Miami

マイアミ

Nyūyōku – New York

ニューヨーク

Hyūsuton – Houston

ヒュ ー スト ン

Detoroito – Detroit

デトロイト

Arasuka – Alaska

アラスカ

Kanada – Canada

カナダ

Bankūbā – Vancouver

バンクーバー

Montoriōru – Montreal

モントリオール

Kebekku – Quebec

ケベック

Toronto – Toronto

トロント

Otawa – Ottawa

オタワ

Mekishiko – Mexico

メキシコ

Mekishikoshitī – Mexico City

メキシコシティー

Europe

Yōroppa – Europe

ヨーロッパ

Furansu – France

フランス

Pari – Paris

パリ

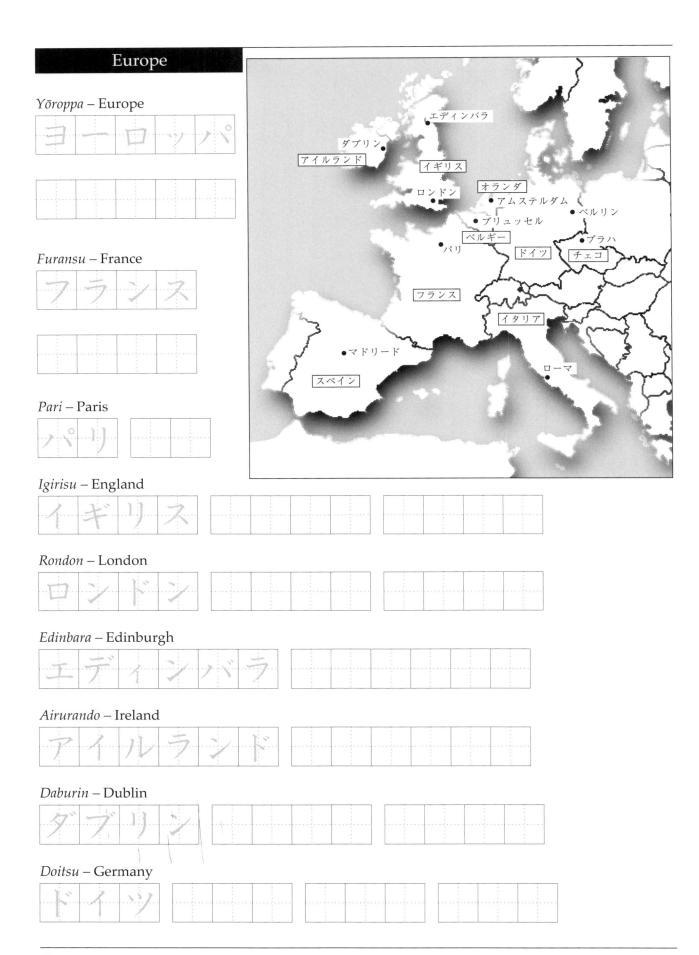

Igirisu – England

イギリス

Rondon – London

ロンドン

Edinbara – Edinburgh

エディンバラ

Airurando – Ireland

アイルランド

Daburin – Dublin

ダブリン

Doitsu – Germany

ドイツ

Berurin – Berlin

ベルリン

Italia – Italy

イタリア

Rōma – Rome

ローマ

Oranda – The Netherlands

オランダ

Amusuterudamu – Amsterdam

アムステルダム

Berugī – Belgium

ベルギー

Buryusseru – Brussels

ブリュッセル

Supein – Spain

スペイン

Madorīdo – Madrid

マドリード

Cheko – The Czech Republic

チェコ

Puraha – Prague

プラハ

Ajia – Asia

ア	ジ	ア

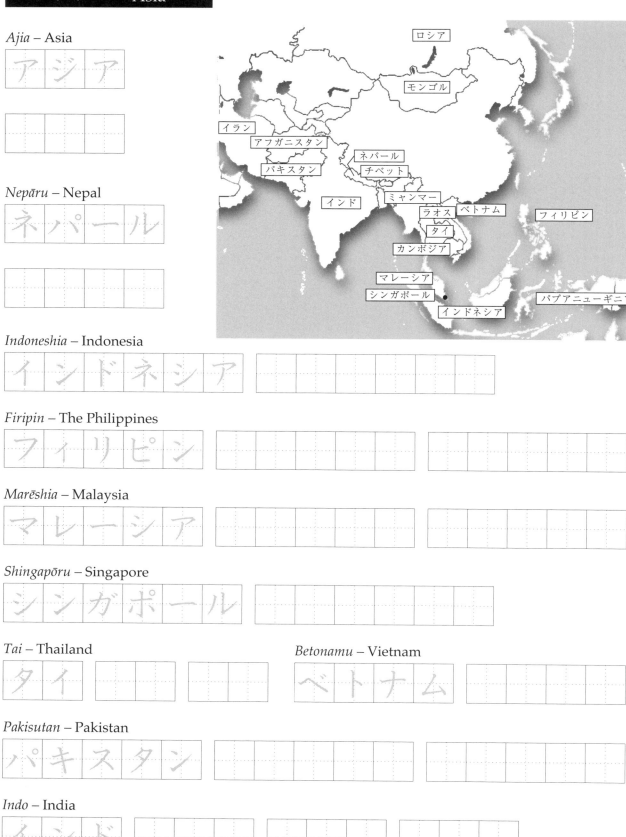

ロシア
モンゴル
イラン
アフガニスタン
ネパール
チベット
パキスタン
インド
ミャンマー
ラオス　ベトナム
タイ
カンボジア
フィリピン
マレーシア
シンガポール
インドネシア
パプアニューギニア

Nepāru – Nepal

ネ	パ	ー	ル

Indoneshia – Indonesia

イ	ン	ド	ネ	シ	ア

Firipin – The Philippines

フ	ィ	リ	ピ	ン

Marēshia – Malaysia

マ	レ	ー	シ	ア

Shingapōru – Singapore

シ	ン	ガ	ポ	ー	ル

Tai – Thailand

タ	イ

Betonamu – Vietnam

ベ	ト	ナ	ム

Pakisutan – Pakistan

パ	キ	ス	タ	ン

Indo – India

イ	ン	ド

Fijī – Fiji

フィジー

Banuatsu – Vanuatu

バヌアツ

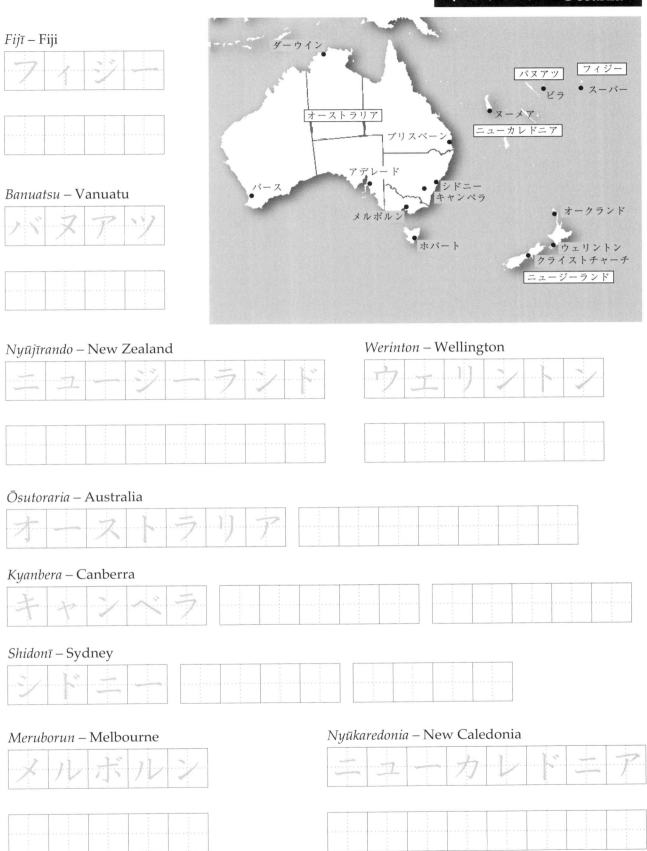

ダーウイン

バヌアツ　フィジー

ビラ　スーバー

オーストラリア

ヌーメア

ニューカレドニア

ブリスベーン

アデレード

パース

シドニー
キャンベラ

メルボルン

オークランド

ホバート

ウェリントン
クライストチャーチ

ニュージーランド

Nyūjīrando – New Zealand

ニュージーランド

Werinton – Wellington

ウェリントン

Ōsutoraria – Australia

オーストラリア

Kyanbera – Canberra

キャンベラ

Shidonī – Sydney

シドニー

Meruborun – Melbourne

メルボルン

Nyūkaredonia – New Caledonia

ニューカレドニア

Fruits & Vegetables

banana – banana

orenji – orange

remon – lemon

mangō – mango

painappuru – pineapple

apurikotto – apricot

meron – melon

cherī – cherry

kiui – kiwi fruit

papaiya – papaya

kokonattsu – coconut

abokado – avocado

raimu – lime

guaba – guava

razuberī – raspberry

burūberī – blueberry

burakkuberī – blackberry

gurēpufurūtsu – grapefruit

グレープフルーツ

karifurawā – cauliflower

カリフラワー

kyabetsu – cabbage

キャベツ

tomato – tomato

トマト

shiitake – shiitake mushroom

シイタケ

serori – celery

セロリ

burokkorī – broccoli

ブロッコリー

asuparagasu – asparagus

アスパラガス

ichijiku – fig

イチジク

retasu – lettuce

レタス

masshurūmu – mushroom

マッシュルーム

pīman – green pepper

ピーマン

zakuro – pomegranate

ザクロ

kureson – watercress

クレソン

puramu – plum

プラム

furaidopoteto – French fries

フライドポテト

ringo – apple

リンゴ

takenoko – bamboo shoot

タケノコ

suika – watermelon

スイカ

tamanegi – onion

タマネギ

ichigo – strawberry

イチゴ

ninniku – garlic

ニンニク

jinjā – ginger

ジンジャー

shōga – ginger

ショウガ

momo – peach

モモ

gobō – burdock

ゴボウ

tōmorokoshi – corn

トウモロコシ

daikon – radish

ダイコン

kyūri – cucumber

キュウリ

ninjin – carrot

ニンジン

maron – (Spanish) chestnut

マロン

kabocha – pumpkin

カボチャ

negi – shallots

ネギ

basukettobōru – basketball

バスケットボール

barēbōru – volleyball

バレーボール

amerikanfuttobōru – American football

アメリカンフットボール

amefuto – American football

アメフト

sunōkeringu – snorkeling

スノーケリング

badominton – badminton

バドミントン

pinpon – table tennis

ピンポン

sukī – skiing

スキー

sakkā – soccer

サッカー

gorufu – golf

ゴルフ

aisuhokkē – ice hockey

アイスホッケー

bodībōdo – body boarding

ボディーボード

sukyūbadaibingu – scuba diving

スキューバダイビング

sāfin – surfing

サーフィン

rirē – relay

リレー

ragubī – rugby

ラグビー

bōringu – ten-pin bowling

ボーリング

bokushingu – boxing

ボクシング

hokkē – hockey

ホッケー

resuringu – wrestling

レスリング

danshingu – dancing

ダンシング

haikingu – hiking

ハイキング

tōnamento – tournament

トーナメント

kuriketto – cricket

クリケット

gēmu – game

ゲーム

ranningu – running

ランニング

sunōbōdo – snowboarding

スノーボード

kyanpu – camping

キャンプ

saikuringu – cycling

サイクリング

earobikusu – aerobics

エアロビクス

tenisu – tennis

テニス

ācherī – archery

アーチェリー

jogingu – jogging

ジョギング

sukēto – skating

スケート

erekigitā – electric guitar

エレキギター

gitā – guitar

ギター

kībōdo – keyboard

キーボート

acōsutikkugitā – acoustic guitar

アコースティックギター

piano – piano

ピアノ

bēsu – bass guitar

ベース

erekibēsu – electric bass

エレキベース

ukurere – ukulele

ウクレレ

basūn – bassoon

バスーン

toranpetto – trumpet

トランペット

pikkoro – piccolo

ピッコロ

konga – conga drums

コンガ

furūto – flute

フルート

horun – French horn

ホルン

sakusofon – saxophone

サクソフォン

kurarinetto – clarinet

クラリネット

furenchihorun – French horn

フレンチホルン

tinpani – timpani

ティンパニ

shinbaru – cymbals

シンバル

baiorin – violin

バイオリン

toraianguru – triangle

トライアングル

hāpu – harp

ハープ

chūba –tuba

チューバ

biora – viola

ビオラ

chero – cello

チェロ

doramu – drums

ドラム

kontorabasu – contrabass

コントラバス

toronbōn – trombone

トロンボーン

ōboe – oboe

オーボエ

rappa – trumpet (general term)

ラッパ

supīkā – speaker

スピーカー

chūnā – tuner

チューナー

maiku – microphone

マイク

metoronōmu – metronome

メトロノーム

sutando – music stand

スタンド

anpu – amplifier

アンプ

dejitarukamera – digital camera

デジタルカメラ

dejikame – digital camera

デジカメ

rajio – radio

ラジオ

bideokamera – video camera

ビデオカメラ

sutereo – stereo

ステレオ

ōbun – oven

オーブン

dībuidīpurēyā – DVD player

DVD プレーヤー

DVD

hottokāpetto – electric carpet

ホットカーペット

kūrā – cooler, air conditioner

クーラー

eakon – air conditioning

エアコン

hītā – heater

ヒーター

tōsutā – toaster

トースター

kōhīmēkā – filtered coffee machine

コーヒーメーカー

mikisā – blender

ミキサー

jūsā – juicer

ジューサー

potto – insulated beverage container

ポット

eakon – aircon / air conditioner

エアコン

terebi – TV

テレビ

denshirenji – microwave oven

でんし　レンジ

でんし　□□□

renji de chin suru – to heat in the microwave

レンジ　で　チン　する

□□□　で　□□　する

massājiki – massage machine

マッサージ　き

□□□□□　き

massājichea – massage chair

マッサージチェア

□□□□□□□

massāji suru – to massage

マッサージ　する

□□□□□　する

kopīki – photocopier

コピー　き

□□□　き

kopī suru – to make a photocopy

コピー　する

□□□　する

sukyanā – scanner

スキャナー

□□□□

sukyan suru – to scan

スキャン　する

□□□　する

fakkusu – fax machine

ファックス

□□□□□

fakkusu suru – to send a fax

ファックス　する

□□□□□　する

denshimēru – email

でんし　メール

でんし　□□□

mēru suru – to send an email

メール　する

□□□　する

kosumechikku – cosmetics

コ ス メ チ ッ ク

kosume – cosmetics

コ ス メ

pakku – facial mask

パ ッ ク

mēkyappu – make up

メ ー キ ャ ッ プ

shanpū – shampoo

シ ャ ン プ ー

rinsu – conditioner

リ ン ス

torītomento – conditioner

ト リ ー ト メ ン ト

handokurīmu – hand cream

ハ ン ド ク リ ー ム

rippukurīmu – lip balm

リ ッ プ ク リ ー ム

manikyua – manicure

マ ニ キ ュ ア

rōshon – lotion

ロ ー シ ョ ン

wakkusu – wax

ワ ッ ク ス

shēbā – shaver

シ ェ ー バ ー

airon – curling iron

ア イ ロ ン

shēbingufōmu – shaving cream

シ ェ ー ビ ン グ フ ォ ー ム

headoraiyā – hairdryer

ヘ ア ド ラ イ ヤ ー

ōrubakku – swept back hair

オールバック

amerikankōhī – weak coffee

アメリカンコーヒー

amerikandoggu – corn dog (frankfurter on a stick dipped, batter and deep-fried)

アメリカンドッグ

bebīkā – pram / stroller

ベビーカー

furontogarasu – windscreen

フロントガラス

saidoburēki – hand brake

サイドブレーキ

gōrudenawā – prime time television

ゴールデンアワー

gādoman – security guard

ガードマン

gēmusentā – game arcade

ゲームセンター

jīnzu – denim (fabric)

ジーンズ

jīpan – jeans

ジーパン

furītā – a person who intentionally works part time

フリーター

sararīman – a male office worker

サラリーマン

risutora – restructuring

リストラ

Harōwāku – unemployment office

ハローワーク

jettokōsutā – roller coaster

ジェットコースター

maipēsu – at one's own pace

マイペース

mainasudoraibā – standard screwdriver

マイナスドライバー

sukinshippu – close relationship

スキンシップ

shāpupenshiru – mechanical/propeling pencil

シャープペンシル

shāpen – mechanical/propeling pencil

シャーペン

wanpatān – repetitive behavior

ワンパターン

pearukku – couple wearing similar clothes

ペアルック

maikā – one's own car

マイカー

shirubāshīto – seat on public transport reserved for elderly passengers

シルバーシート

sofutokurīmu – soft serve confection

ソフトクリーム

rabuhoteru – hourly-rate hotel (used by couples for short stay)

ラブホテル

baikingu – buffet

バイキング

maihōmu – one's own home

マイホーム

supīdodaun – slow down

スピードダウン

apointo – appointment

アポイント

apo – appointment

アポ

kuraianto – client

クライアント

sutaffu – staff member(s)

スタッフ

sērusu – sales

セールス

kasutamā – customer

カスタマー

demonsutorēshon – (product) demonstration

デモンストレーション

intānetto – internet

インターネット

sekyuritī – security

セキュリティー

purezentēshon – presentation

プレゼンテーション

manējā – manager

マネージャー

mēkā – manufacturer

メーカー

pāto – part-time worker

パート

roguin – login

ログイン

kosuto – cost

コスト

chēnsutoa – chain store

チェーンストア

afutāsābisu – after-sales service

アフターサービス

autoretto – factory outlet

アウトレット

haiteku – high-tech

ハイテク

ōdā – order

オーダー

purojekuto – project

プロジェクト

katarogu – catalog

カタログ

kurēmu – customer complaint

クレーム

kyanpēn – campaign

キャンペーン

furanchaizu – franchise

フランチャイズ

māketingu – marketing

マーケティング

panfuretto – pamphlet

パンフレット

sanpuru – sample

サンプル

baiyā – buyer

バイヤー

mentenansu – maintenance

メンテナンス

yūzā – user

ユーザー

burando – brand

ブランド

kyanseru – cancel

キャンセル

Internet Slang

appu suru – to upload

アップ する

する

komento suru – to comment

コメント する

する

otaku – geek

オタク

kopipe suru – to copy and paste

コピペ する

する

shea suru – to share

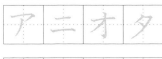

シェア する

する

guguru– to Google

ググ る

る

anison – anime song
(abbreviated)

アニソン

aniota – anime geek
(abbreviation of *anime otaku*)

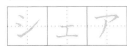

アニオタ

anime – anime /
Japanese animation

アニメ

insutōru suru – to install (software)

インストール する

する

gujjobu – good job

グッジョブ

neta – a joke / story

ネタ

imetagu – tag on a photo (abbreviation of 'image tag')

イメタグ

warota – online term for 'laugh'

ワロタ

apuri – smartphone app

アプリ

ikemen – good looking

イケメン

kosupure – cosplay

コスプレ

sureddo – online thread

スレッド

tagu suru – to tag

タグ する

する

daunrōdo suru – to download

ダウンロード する

する

taimurain – timeline (on Facebook)

タイムライン

tsuīto – tweet

ツイート

deriru – to delete

デリ る

る

baguru – to infect a computer with a virus

バグ る

る

hakku suru – to hack

ハック する

する

figyua – an action figure

フィギュア

forō suru – to follow

フォロー する

する

hikkī – a recluse (abbreviation of *hikikomori*)

ヒッキー

mēru – email

メール

meruado – email address (abbreviated)

メルアド

kimoi – yuck (abbreviation of *kimochiwarui*)

キモイ

tsundere – pretense of emotional detachment (abbreviation of *tsun tsun dere dere*)

ツンデレ

resu – response (abbreviated) to messages or comments on social networking sites

レス

A

abokado - avocado
ācherī - archery
acōsutikkugitā - acoustic guitar
afutāsābisu - after-sales service
aidoru - popular famous person
airon - curling iron
Airurando - Ireland
aisuhokkē - ice hockey
aisukōhī - iced coffee
Ajia - Asia
ākedo - arcade
akua - aqua
akusesu - access
akushon - action (movie)
amefuto - American football
Amerika - America
amerikandoggu - corn dog (frankfurter on a stick dipped, batter and deep-fried)
amerikanfuttobōru - American football
amerikankōhī - weak coffee
Amusuterudamu - Amsterdam
Andoryū - Andrew
anime - anime/Japanese animation
aniota - anime geek (abbreviation of anime otaku)
anison - anime song (abbreviated)
ankēto - questionnaire
anpu - amplifier
Ansonī - Anthony
apāto - Japanese-style apartment
apo - appointment
apointo - appointment
appu - improvement (used as a suffix)
appu suru - to upload
apuri - smartphone app
apurikotto - apricot
Arasuka - Alaska
Arekisandā - Alexander
arubaito - part-time work
Ashurī - Ashley/Ashleigh
asuparagasu - asparagus
Atoranta - Atlanta
atorie - artist's studio
autoretto - factory outlet

B

badominton - badminton
baguru - to infect a computer with a virus
baikingu - buffet
baiorin - violin
baiyā - buyer
baketsu - bucket
banana - banana
Bankūbā - Vancouver
Banuatsu - Vanuatu
barēbōru - volleyball
baree - ballet
basha basha - sound of legs kicking in a pool
basu - bus
basukettobōru - basketball
basūn - bassoon
batā - butter
batan - the sound of a door slamming

batto - bat
bebīkā - pram/stroller
Benjamin - Benjamin
Berugī - Belgium
Berurin - Berlin
bēsu - bass guitar
Betonamu - Vietnam
bideo - video
bideokamera - video camera
biora - viola
bīru - beer
biru - building, office block
bisuketto - biscuit
biza - visa
bodībōdo - body boarding
bokushingu - boxing
borantia - charity work
bōringu - ten-pin bowling
boryūmu - (sound) volume
Bosuton - Boston
buku buku - the sound of water boiling
burakkuberī - blackberry
burando - brand
buranko - playground swings
burokkorī - broccoli
burūberī - blueberry
Buryusseru - Brussels

C

Cheko - The Czech Republic
chēnsutoa - chain store
cherī - cherry
chero - cello
chesu - chess
chikutaku - the sound of a clock ticking
chin - the sound of a bell on a microwave
chīzu - cheese
chokorēto - chocolate
chūba - tuba
chū chū - the sound of a mouse squeaking
chūnā - tuner

D

Daburin - Dublin
Dābī - Derby
daibā - diver
daietto - diet
daikon - radish
danshingu - dancing
daunrōdo suru - to download
Dāwin - Darwin
Dēbiddo - David
dejikame - digital camera
dejitarukamera - digital camera
demonsutorēshon - (product) demonstration
denshimēru - email
densirenji - microwave
depāto - department store
deriru - to delete
dēta - data
Detoroito - Detroit
dībuidīpurēyā - DVD player
Diran - Dylan
direkutā - director
Doitsu - Germany
dokān - the sound of a cannon booming
doki doki - the sound of a

heart beating
doramu - drums
doru - dollar

E

eakon - airconditioning
earobikusu - aerobics
Edinbara - Edinburgh
ēkā - acre
Emirī - Emily
enerugī - energy
erekibēsu - electric bass
erekigitā - electric guitar
ēsu - ace (tennis, cards)

F

fakkusu - fax machine
fakkusu suru - to fax
fasshon - fashion
fenikkusu - Phoenix
figyua - an action figure
Fijī - Fiji
fikushon - fiction
Firentse - Florence (Firenze)
Firipin - The Philippines
firumu - (a roll of) film
fōku - fork
forō suru - to follow
furaidopoteto - French fries
furanchaizu - franchise
Furansu - France
furenchihorun - French horn
furītā - a person who intentionally works part time
furonto - hotel reception desk
furontogarasu - windscreen
furūto - flute

G

Gaburieru - Gabriel
gabu gabu - the sound of a person gulping
gachan - the sound of glass breaking
gādoman - security guard
gaō - a lion roaring
garasu - glass (as a substance)
gārikku - garlic
gāze - bandage, gauze
gēmu - game
gēmusentā - game arcade
gerende - ski slope (Gel‰nde - German)
giko giko - the sound of a saw cutting
gitā - guitar
gobō - burdock
gomu - rubber
gōruden'awā - prime time television
Gōrudenwīku - Golden Week holidays
gorufu - golf
goshi goshi - the sound of a scrubbing brush
guaba - guava
guguru - to Google
gujjobu - good job
gurasu - glass, tumbler
guriru - grill
gurēpufurūtsu - grapefruit
gurōbu - baseball or boxing glove
gurururu - the sound of a stomach rumbling
gyararī - gallery

H

haikā - hiker
haikingu - hiking
haiteku - high-tech
hakku suru - to hack
hakkushon - the sound of a person sneezing
hāmonika - harmonica
handokurīmu - hand cream
handoru - steering wheel
Hanna - Hannah
hāpu - harp
Harōwāku - unemployment office
headoraiyā - hairdryer
hihīn - the sound of a horse neighing
hikkī - a recluse (abbreviation of hikikomori)
hītā - heater
hokkē - hockey
hōmu - railway platform
hōmuran - home run
horun - French horn
Hosē - Jose
hotto kāpetto - electric carpet
hyū - the sound of the wind blowing
Hyūsuton - Houston
hyūzu - fuse

I

ichigo - strawberry
ichijiku - fig
Igirisu - England
ikemen - good looking
imetagu - tag on a photo (abbreviation of 'image tag')
Indo - India
Indoneshia - Indonesia
infomēshon - information
insutōru suru - to install
intabyū - interview
intāchenji - interchange
intānashonaru - international, American
intānetto - internet
Italia - Italy
Izabera - Isabella

J

jā - water gushing out of a tap
jānarisuto - journalist
Jasumin - Jasmine
Jasutin - Justin
Jeikobu - Jacob
Jēmuzu - James
Jenifā - Jennifer
Jeshika - Jessica
jettokōsutā - roller coaster
jiguzagu - zigzag
jinjā - ginger
jīnzu - denim
jīpan - jeans
jogingu - jogging
joki joki - the sound of scissors snipping
Jon - John
Josefu - Joseph
Juria - Julia
jūsā - juicer
jūsu - juice, uncarbonated soft drink

K

kā kā - the sound of a crow squawking
kabocha - pumpkin
kafeore - café au lait

Kairī - Kylie
kajuaru - casual
kāki iro - khaki (color)
kakīn - a baseball bat hitting a ball
kameraman - photographer
Kanada - Canada
kangarū - kangaroo
kanū - canoe
kapuchino - cappuccino
karā - color
karaoke - a sing-along machine
karendā - calendar
karifurawā - cauliflower
kāru - curl or Carl
karuchāshokku - culture chock
karutetto - quartet
kasettotēpu - cassette tape
kāsoru - cursor
kasutamā - customer
katarogu - catalog
katto - cut
Kebekku - Quebec
kēki - cake
kero kero - the sound of a frog croaking
kēsu - case
kī - the sound of chalk, tires squeaking
kībōdo - keyboard(s)
kira kira - twinkling or sparkling
kiro - kilogram or kilometer
kisu - kiss
kiui - kiwi fruit
koara - koala
kōhī - coffee
kōhīmēkā - filtered coffee machine
kokekokkō - the sound of a rooster crowing
kokoa - cocoa
kokonattsu - coconut
komāsharu - (TV/radio) commercial
kimoi- yuck (abbreviation of kimochiwarui)
komento suru - to comment
konga - conga drums
konpyūtā - computer
konsento - power point, wall socket
kontakutorenzu - contact lens
kontorabasu - contrabass
kopī suru - to photocopy
kopīki - photocopier
kopipe suru - to copy and paste
koppu - glass, tumbler
kosume - cosmetics
kosumechikku - cosmetics
kosupure - cosplay
kosuto - cost
kuēkā - Quaker
kuizu - quiz
kūrā - cooler, air conditioner
kuraianto - client
kurakushon - car horn
kurarinetto - clarinet
kurēmu - customer complaint
kureson - watercress
kuriketto - cricket